BETTER BUSINESS COMMUNICATION

A *QUICK* GUIDE TO

EMAIL, PRESENTATIONS, TELEPHONE SKILLS, WRITING & GRAMMAR

HEATHER WRIGHT

Heather Wright
hwrightwriter@gmail.com

Book Layout ©2013 BookDesignTemplates.com

Better Business Communication
A QUICK GUIDE TO:
Email, Presentations, Telephone Skills, Writing & Grammar
/ Heather Wright. —1st ed.

Saugeen Publishers

This book is a compilation of four books in the **Better Business Communication** series. In it, you will find the complete texts of the following:

A Quick Guide to Better Emails

A Quick Guide to Better Presentations

A Quick Guide to Better Telephone Skills

A Quick Guide to Better Writing and Grammar

Contents

A QUICK GUIDE TO WRITING BETTER EMAILS

Introduction

This book is **your quick guide to writing better emails**. Ten short chapters outline the strategies you need for writing emails that get the responses you want and mark you as a professional.

People spend a lot of time on their computers or smartphones communicating for fun. Facebook, Twitter, and instant messaging have made us very fond of short forms, acronyms and multiple punctuation marks!!! But business writing is different.

Writing for business has two purposes:
1. **to make your company look good.**
2. **to make you look good.**

In ancient times, such as those when I first went to work in an office, managers had secretaries. Managers dictated letters and secretaries typed them up, corrected the grammar, and were responsible for accurate spelling and formatting.

Those days are gone. There is no skilled buffer between your thoughts and the words that go to your clients, co-workers, and your boss.

And the pace has changed, too. Letters could be proofread, retyped, and changed again, before they were finally put in the mailbox at the end of the day. The recipient knew that it could take a week before he or she got the answer to the original letter.

Business today would collapse with that kind of time line. The expectation is that email gets answered within a matter of hours or even parts of hours. **Quick response is expected**.

Your limited time is the reason that this book is short. You don't have the time to muddle through a large text. You need quick fixes fast. Read this book from the beginning or just read the chapters that apply to the questions you have now.

CHAPTER 1

Making the Subject Line Do Its Job

The subject line gets your email opened, so it needs to do its job. Subject lines need to be clear and also have enough information in them to help the recipient prioritize his or her response.

Let's face it; email boxes fill up quickly. If you want an answer to your email, you have to let your reader know your email's purpose right away. No cute half sentences to make the reader open the email to read the rest. No silly references to sex or money to trick the reader into opening the mail. No "You won't want to miss this!!!"

Your email subject line should be an effective summary of the email's contents with enough information for the reader to decide if it's urgent or not. And please don't bother to mark your email *urgent*. If an issue really is urgent, pick up the phone. Half of your reader's correspondents think their emails are urgent, too. After a while, it gets to be very easy to ignore those red exclamation marks.

Let's have a look at some examples.

Example 1

You are asking your co-workers to complete a short survey to help HR choose next year's benefits package. Here are some options that will get your request ignored and one that will likely work:

Re: HR Survey
Reader response: Another one? Don't have time for this.

Re: Benefits
Reader response: I'll look at that later.

Re: Benefits Survey
Reader response: I'll look at that later.

Re: Short Survey for Your 2016 Benefits' Package Due April 4th
Reader response: I'd better do that now before I forget. This subject line works for a couple of reasons. 1) Using the word "your" takes the topic away from the impersonal. Completing the survey will directly affect the reader. 2) A date is mentioned. The reader is more likely to respond if he or she knows that the time for input is limited. 3) The word "short" is encouraging. The reader feels he or

she can take the time to do it now, without losing too much valuable time.

Example 2

You've discovered an excellent online course on warehouse management that you want to take. A couple of your co-workers have already taken it and found it very valuable. You have to write to the boss to ask for funding for the course. Here are some options that will get your request ignored and one that will likely work:

Re: Online Course
Reader response: Haven't a clue what that's about. I'll leave it until later.

Re: Request for Online Course
Reader response: Does he/she want to take one of the company courses? Someone else's? I'll leave it until later.

Re: Requesting Funding for Warehouse Management Online Course
Reader response: I remember that course. Bill and Maria took it. Very valuable. Let's get this cleared away now.

IN SHORT

Email subject lines should

- Use capital letters on all words except short prepositions and conjunctions. (See samples above.)
- Give the reader enough information to be able to decide how to prioritize his or her response.
- Include a date if the response has to be timely.
- Avoid jokes, lots of punctuation, and vague statements or teasers.

CHAPTER 2

The Salutation—Saying Hello

Email resembles letters in many ways, but since so few people write letters, it's worthwhile to remind you about salutations.

Always begin your email message with a greeting. Here are some examples:

- *Hi,* or *Hi Harriet,*
- *Dear Harriet,* - use the recipient's first name, if you know the person, or if that's the way they signed their email to you.
- *Dear Mr. Wilson,* - use a more formal approach, if the person is a stranger or if you are aware that the person has influence in your company. When you are writing to senior management, especially if the person is older, a more formal approach is usually more appropriate.
- Never write Dear Mr. Jim Wilson. The correct salutations are either Dear Jim or Dear Mr. Wilson.
- Another method is to use the person's name in the first sentence, for example:

Thanks, Bill, for getting back to me so quickly. Use commas on either side of the person's name to punctuate your sentence correctly.

IN SHORT

- Always use a salutation or include the recipient's name in the first sentence.
- Hi, Dear First Name, or Dear Surname are your best choices followed by a comma.

CHAPTER 3

Begin with the Purpose

If you are writing an email that is delivering information, or asking a question, or thanking someone, there's no need to keep the purpose a secret. Putting the purpose of your email in the first paragraph is just fine.

If you know that the person has been away sick or is coming back from vacation, it's okay to make a one line reference to that, as well.

Here are a couple of examples.

Example 1

Dear Leslie,

Welcome back from holidays. I hope you had a great time in Florida.

While you were away, several changes were made to the Benson contract. Here's a summary of the changes that we will be discussing at Friday's meeting ... *and the rest of the email lists the changes to the contract.*

Example 2

Thanks for getting back to me so quickly, Micah. I've thought of one more question since we last spoke. Which date did the client agree upon for the final payment?

In the first example, the email could have started fine without the reference to the holidays. In the second example, the information needed is referred to in the first paragraph.

IN SHORT

Without being too abrupt or curt, get to the point of your email early. With so many emails landing in people's mailboxes these days, readers have a tendency to skim in an effort to move through their mailbox quickly. Get your information up front before your reader's attention wanders.

CHAPTER 4

Building the Message

Email is broken into short paragraphs for a couple of reasons. 1) A new paragraph is required for a new topic. 2) Short paragraphs separated by empty lines look a lot more reader-friendly and inviting on the screen than a dense block of text.

A Note about Grammar and Spelling

The sentences in your paragraphs should be complete. They should begin with a capital letter and end with a period. Your spelling should be correct. The purpose of correct grammar and spelling is to make your writing look professional and for your message to be as accessible and easy-to-read as possible. If a client or your boss has to reread a sentence a couple of times to figure out what you are saying, the response to your email might just reflect his or her frustration.

Correct punctuation and use of capitals tells your reader that you care about the quality of your work. It may seem like a small thing, but **it**

builds trust. Imagine if you are a financial planner writing to your client. If you don't take the time to make sure that the spelling and grammar of your message are correct, why should the client trust that you would take care of the details in his or her financial plan?

The Middle of the Message

After you have explained the purpose of the email, the middle paragraph or paragraphs are used to add more details that your reader might need in order to make a decision. **Use a new paragraph for each new topic**. If you have several points to cover or pieces of information to deliver, consider using a bulleted list. The **Rules for Bulleted Lists are in Chapter 6**.

If you are responding to a list of questions or concerns, **copy the list of questions or concerns from the original email into your reply**, and answer each one, typing your answer below the question. If you do this, you will ensure that you have answered all the questions or addressed all the concerns that were sent in the original email. Preface your list with the words *Here are the answers to the questions you sent on Tuesday.*

Here's how the letter begun in step 3 might continue:

Dear Leslie,

Welcome back from holidays. I hope you had a great time in Florida.

While you were away, several changes were made to the Benson contract. Here's a summary of the changes that we will be discussing at Friday's meeting:

1. Paragraph 4 – Parker Co. is changed to Parker Company. This change is continued throughout the contract.
2. Paragraph 12 – The sum of restitution has been changed to $20,000 from $10,000.
3. Paragraphs 20 to 30 – Note the changes here to the partnership agreement requested by Helen.
4. Paragraph 42 – Note the change to insurance coverage that has been requested by Helen.

IN SHORT

- Use short paragraphs.
- Each paragraph should deal with a new topic.
- Make sure that spelling and grammar are correct.
- Copy questions from the original email into your reply and answer each one.

CHAPTER 5

Writing the Ending

The last paragraph of an email is the place where you insert the call to action (if necessary), wrap up your message, and say thanks or that you are looking forward to hearing from the recipient again.

The end of an email includes a complimentary close. These tend to be short and include the following:

Best regards,

Regards,

Yours truly,

Sincerely,

The complimentary close should be followed by your first name and your email signature that includes your full name, your position with the company, your email address, and your phone number. You can set these up on your email program to be added automatically to all of your correspondence. The end of the message begun in Step 3 might look like this:

Dear Leslie,

Welcome back from holidays. I hope you had a great time in Florida.

While you were away, several changes were made to the Benson contract. Here's a summary of the changes that we will be discussing at Friday's meeting:

1. Paragraph 4 – Parker Co. is changed to Parker Company. This change is continued throughout the contract.
2. Paragraph 12 – The sum of restitution has been changed to $20,000 from $10,000.
3. Paragraphs 20 to 30 – Note the changes here to the partnership agreement requested by Helen.
4. Paragraph 42 – Note the change to insurance coverage that has been requested by Helen.

I look forward to seeing you on Friday and hearing your views on the above changes. If you have any questions in the meantime, please give me a call at ext. 32.

Best regards,

Heather

Heather Wright
Vice-President
555-123-4567 ext. 89
hwright@thecompany.com

IN SHORT

- Include a complimentary close.
- Set up an email signature to include all necessary contact info.
- Include a call to action in the final paragraph and mention how you can be contacted.

CHAPTER 6

Cutting the Fat

Here are some tricks for cutting the fat in your email correspondence. In order to sound formal and serious, writers often resort to padding their messages with a lot of unnecessary words. When in doubt, apply the KISS principle: keep it short and simple.

Example

Wordy—107 words

Dear Eleanor,

It has come to my attention, that our esteemed client, Bill Hawkins, is celebrating a 15-year anniversary with our company. I believe that it would be appropriate and also a gesture of our company's goodwill and thanks for his loyalty through those years, if we offered him an invitation to our company's golf tournament. I would appreciate your letting me know, as soon as it is feasible, whether it will be possible or not to add Bill's name to the list for the tournament.

Once again, I appreciate your looking into this matter for me, and I look forward to hearing from you soon.

Regards,

Not So Wordy – 53 words

Dear Eleanor,

Bill Hawkins has been a great client for 15 years. To say thank-you for his loyalty, I'd like to invite him to our company golf tournament. Please let me know whether I can invite Bill. I'd like to let him know by Friday.

Thanks for looking into this for me.

Regards,

For a simple request such as the one above, there's no reason to be anything but brief and to the point. In both cases, we know that Bill is a valuable client, and in both cases, we know that the writer wants to invite him to the company golf tournament. And you can still use the magic words, please and thank you.

Below are some tips for eliminating wordiness in your writing. For more information, check:

http://leo.stcloudstate.edu/style/wordiness.html

http://www.grammarly.com/blog/2015/make-your-writing-clearer-6-tips-for-re-wording-sentencesa/

1. Eliminate Qualifiers
Sentences are rarely improved by the addition of words such as extremely, really, and very. Find a better adjective to replace phrases with those words in them or just leave them out entirely.
Extremely sad – sad, crushed, despondent, bereft, grief-stricken
Very happy – happy, cheerful, overjoyed, delirious, thrilled
Really hungry – hungry, starving, ravenous, famished
Very angry – angry, livid, furious, apoplectic …

2. Eliminate There is, Here is, There was, It was, It is, There will be, It will be
These words can usually be dropped from the beginnings of sentences.

There were ten people waiting in line ahead of me.
Ten people were ahead of me in line.

It was an informative meeting.
The meeting was informative.

There will be a meeting at noon tomorrow.
The meeting is at noon tomorrow.

3. Combine sentences that repeat the same information.

The meeting is a noon tomorrow. We will be meeting in the boardroom to discuss the new pension plan.
The meeting to discuss the new pension plan is at noon tomorrow in the boardroom.

I just spoke to Bill. He talked about the new system of keeping track of accounts. He said the new system would be faster to learn.
Bill said the new system of keeping track of accounts would be faster to learn.

4. Eliminate longer phrases and replace with shorter words.

I've included a few examples below, so you can see what I mean. To see a more comprehensive list check here:
http://writing.wisc.edu/Handbook/CCS_wordyphrases.html

In order to meet the deadline ….
To meet the deadline ….

In consideration of the fact that the weather will be cold in January ….
Because the weather will be cold in January ….

At this moment in time, it's important to remember….
Now, it's ….
Today ….

IN SHORT

- Eliminate flowery, too formal language
- Eliminate qualifiers.
- Eliminate Here is, There is, etc.
- Combine sentences that contain the same information
- Eliminate longer phrases and replace with shorter words

CHAPTER 7

Rules for Bullet Lists

Lists are a very efficient way to present information in your email, but they need to have a very specific format. Use bullets when listing a series of items. Use numbers when listing a set of steps that have to be followed in order or to prioritize the list by ranking the information in order.

Rules for the Lead In

If the lead-in that precedes the list is a complete sentence, you end it with a colon.

Examples

The following are the four points I'd like you to consider:

Here are the 5 steps you need to follow:

Please answer the following questions:

The material required includes the following:

If the lead-in is not a complete sentence, that means that the material following the lead-in is completing the sentence; therefore, the lead-in has no punctuation after it.

Examples

The four steps require to complete this project are

It's important to remember that

I'd appreciate your input on

Rules for Punctuation

Here are a couple of examples that show how the rest of the list is punctuated.

Example 1

Please complete the following and return them to me by Friday:

- Status Form 1303
- Standard Release 12
- Personnel Questionnaire
- Tax Form C39.

Example 2

In order to be ready for the meeting, you will need to

- review the Benson contract,
- bring tax information relating to the Morris partnership, and
- review the Hendley incorporation documents.

Note that in the above example, the list is punctuated as if it were written out as one long sentence with commas after the items in the list. It would look like the following:

In order to be ready for the meeting, you will need to review the Benson contract, bring tax information relating to the Morris partnership, and review the Hendley incorporation documents.

Rules for the contents

All of the items in the list need to follow the same pattern. In Example 2, all of the items in the list are nouns/things. In Example 2, every point begins with a verb/action: review, bring, review.

Here's an example of a list in which the items don't follow the same pattern.

On Friday morning
- Bring your laptop
- Go to meeting room B
- You'll need a 2G memory stick.

In the above example, the first two items begin with verbs (bring, go) and the third item is a sentence starting with the pronoun, you. Since all the items in the list need to match, the third item also needs to start with a verb.

On Monday morning
- bring your laptop
- go to meeting room B
- bring an empty 2G memory stick.

Here are two more before and after examples. When you write your lists correctly, it's called parallel construction.

When winter comes, we love to
- ski
- make snowmen
- skate in the park
- making snow angels at Grandma's house.

When winter comes, we love to
- ski
- make snowmen
- skate in the park
- make snow angels at Grandma's house.

Here are some steps you need to complete in order to write a report:
- Brainstorm ideas
- Find research sources
- Draft an outline
- Writing the first draft comes next.

Here are some steps you need to complete in order to write a report:
- Brainstorm ideas
- Find research sources
- Draft an outline
- Write the first draft.

IN SHORT

- If the lead-in is a complete sentence, it is followed by a colon.
- The items in a list preceded by a colon begin with a capital letter. If they are single words or phrases, they need no end punctuation. If they are short sentences, each sentence needs a period at the end.
- If the lead-in is not a complete sentence, no punctuation is required.
- The items in a list following an incomplete sentence do not begin with a capital letter and are followed by commas with a period at the end—as if you were writing it out as one long sentence.
- All items in the list need to follow the same format—parallel construction

CHAPTER 8

If You Are Asking for Something

Request letters generally follow the same format. In the **first paragraph**, explain what you are requesting. Put yourself in the reader's shoes. Think about what *you* would need to know before you could say yes or no the request. Include as much of the relevant information as possible to make the recipient's decision easier.

In the example below, the key to getting a positive response is to make sure that you are very clear about what you are asking for. The writer here has given Barney enough information to make a decision. Barney knows the time, the purpose, and the duration of the event.

In the **second paragraph**, offer the recipient more information or background to the request.

In the **concluding paragraph**, make sure that the recipient knows where to get more information and how he or she should reply to the request. If there is a deadline, make sure that it is clear to the recipient, so that you have enough time to contact someone else if the first person says no.

Example

Hi Barney,

I have been looking for a speaker for our next managers' lunch meeting, and Helen suggested that you would be a good person to ask. The hour-long meeting is on February 9 at 12:30 in the Atlantic board room, and the focus of the meeting is *meeting goals*. Our speakers usually talk for about fifteen minutes, and another ten minutes is set aside for questions. Helen said that we could learn a lot from you and how you achieved your goal of walking 2013 kilometers in 2013 and 2014 kilometers in 2014.

I'm sure the managers would be very interested to learn how you approached such a big task and how you overcame any problems. Our meetings are informal and lunch is provided.

Please let me know by January 17, if you can speak to our group. If you have any questions, please call me at extension 459. I look forward to hearing from you.

Sincerely,

Heather

Heather Wright
Vice-President
555-123-4567 ext. 89
hwright@thecompany.com

IN SHORT

- Explain what you are asking for at the beginning.
- Give the reader all the details he or she needs to make a decision.
- Make sure that the reader has two ways to contact you with his or her response.

CHAPTER 9

Email Etiquette

Email is a challenging medium. You need to respond quickly, write well, and make sure that you and your business look good.

Here are some suggestions to help make sure that the last item on the above list is guaranteed.

Skip the sarcasm and humor

Email is the most misunderstood medium of communication. What gets in the way of email doing its job well is the lack of context that the reader has when decoding the message. What you might think is great sarcasm or a witty remark, your reader can find insulting or hurtful. It's best just to stick with the facts and remember to say please and thank you. Check the link below to learn more about email and miscommunication.

https://www.psychologytoday.com/blog/contemp orary-psychoanalysis-in-action/201502/why-is-there-so-much-miscommunication-email-and

Why Is There So Much Miscommunication Via Email and Text? How we interpret electronic messages is shaped by our feelings

Post published by <u>The Contemporary Psychoanalysis Group</u> on Feb 15, 2015 in <u>Contemporary Psychoanalysis in Action</u>

Style and Form

Terse incomplete sentences with spelling errors do not send the message that you are busy or too important to worry about writing correctly. You wouldn't expect to receive a message in that format from a junior employee, so why would you set the example of bad writing for all to see.

Use email to model professional standards that you want your employees to emulate when they are writing to customers. Even if your boss writes messages like this, there is no need for you to copy him or her.

FULL CAPS

Skip using full caps in your emails. When words are in full caps it means they are being shouted. You wouldn't shout at clients and co-workers in real life (though, I know it could be tempting), so don't do it on paper.

IN SHORT

- Don't try to be funny or use sarcasm.
- Always use correct spelling, grammar, and punctuation.
- Full Caps shout at your reader—don't use them

CHAPTER 10

Bulk Mail Tricks and EOM

Bulk Mail

Bulk mail needs to be handled with care. If you are sending a notice about a new product to a group of your clients, use the BCC box to enter their email addresses and put only your address in the TO box.

When you put all of your clients' email addresses in the TO box, every person that receives your message can also see the names and addresses of your other clients. Some of your clients might not appreciate having their email addresses shared, and others might not want everyone else to know that they are your client, especially if they are also working with other people in the field.

When you put their addresses into the BCC box, they only see your address and theirs. You maintain their privacy and save the time of creating separate emails.

EOM – End of Message

Using EOM is a time saver for everyone.

When you want to thank someone quickly, write your thank-you message in the subject line and end with EOM. For example, if someone has sent you links to some important information, you could reply and change the subject line to *Thanks for the great information. EOM.* When the person sees EOM, he or she knows that they don't have to open the email to read the message. You've put the message in the subject line.

If you and many others are invited to an event, don't click reply all. Just reply and change the subject line to include your acceptance of the invitation. Looking forward to the meeting on the 22nd. EOM

IN SHORT

- Use BCC to hide the names of all the recipients in a bulk mailing.
- Use EOM to put your short message in the subject line and to save your reader's time.

A QUICK GUIDE TO BETTER PRESENTATIONS

Introduction

This book is **your quick guide to better presentations**. In ten short chapters, you'll have the strategies you need to create viewer-friendly presentations and to develop the speaking skills you need to mark you as a professional.

Like every other form of business communication, **presentations have two purposes:**

1. to make your company look good.
2. to make you look good.

This book will refer to PowerPoint® presentations but you can extrapolate the guidelines to any presentation format you choose. A format that adds more movement to your presentation or has backgrounds that are more interesting isn't necessarily more accessible or more appreciated by your audience.

If you're going to apply the KISS principle (*Keep It Short and Simple*) to any form of business communication, your presentation is the one to pick. The strategies that follow will help you make a good impression and avoid boring your audience, and give you a pattern to follow that will make you a sought after presenter.

CHAPTER 1

Tip 1: Planning

To start planning your presentation, here are some questions you should ask:

- What's the purpose of my presentation? To explain, sell, lead a discussion, teach a concept?
- Who is my audience? How much does my audience know about the subject of my presentation already? (We'll look more closely at the topic of audience in Chapter 2.)
- How much time have I been allotted?
- What setting will I be in? Board room with senior management? Auditorium with 300 people? Meeting room with ten or twenty people? Will they be eating? Are they expected to take notes?

The purpose of your presentation affects several things.

If you're explaining or describing a new product or a change in company policy, you'll need to make sure that your audience goes home with written material to refer to later. If the topic is complex, your job is not to make it more so. Think about how you can simplify the material into as few slides as possible to give the audience an over view, and allow them the time to ask questions or talk to you later about details they have discovered in the written material.

If the content could be upsetting to your audience (bad news regarding layoffs or a decrease in company benefits) most of your time should be spent talking to the people in the room and showing empathy rather than flashing a series of slides at them. For them, the information you are passing on will change their lives. Being present as a person is more important than the history of the company's slide to insolvency.

If you are there to lead a discussion or a brainstorming session, your slides should do no more than provide talking points.

If you are teaching a concept, make sure that your slides contain more than just bullet points, which your audience will read before you have addressed each one and then doze off to wait for the next one. Make sure that you find ways in the teaching time to get the audience involved. Break them into groups for short discussions or for hands-on trials of the points you are teaching. Nothing teaches better than hands-on learning.

With regard to the time you have allotted to you, please **ignore the old standby of one slide per minute.** You've sat through enough of these presentations yourself to know that it's a recipe for boredom, information overload, and surreptitious viewing of smartphones as an escape mechanism. Your job is to inform and entertain, where possible, but never to bore. We'll talk about how to work around this rule in Chapter 3.

Your setting influences the appearance of your slides, too. If you are addressing an auditorium full of people, bullet points are lost on the back row. Unless the hall is completely dark, the chance of people being able to read your material is slim.

Look for visuals that summarize or highlight your points. Your slides serve more to emphasize what you are saying rather than contain everything you are saying. If you have a group of people in a smaller room or around a board table, make sure that your slides work with the lights on in the room and that you allow time for discussion and audience involvement to ensure engagement.

IN SHORT

- Plan your presentation based on its purpose.
- Ignore the 1 slide/minute rule.

- Consider setting when designing the content of your slides.

CHAPTER 2

Tip 2: Thinking of the Audience

Consider who your audience is and **how much they know already.** If the information you are presenting is new to them, more background may be required.

Think about the age of your audience. Senior management may not appreciate your LOL references or what you might think are humorous comparisons to current pop musicians.

How many other presentations has your audience already sat through before yours? If your presentation is part of a series at an information day or conference, you need to find a way for your material and your presentation to stand out. You have competition for your audience's attention. As soon as the screen lights up, they're inwardly (or maybe not) rolling their eyes at yet another sixty PowerPoint® slides. What can you do that is different?

How early did they get up to drive to your presentation? Coffee can't solve everything, and since, at conferences, coffee is usually served with sugary treats, expect a sugar slump about 30 minutes into your presentation. What can you schedule at that time to keep your audience awake? Can you work in an activity where they have to get up and move or talk to a neighbor or gather in a group or solve a puzzle or ... you get the idea.

Does your audience have to be there? Has management told them that they have to attend? If they are there because they have to be there, you might have a little hostility to overcome. They are likely leaving a desk-load of work behind, knowing that emails are pinging in all the time you are speaking that they will have to catch up on later

Be genuine in your appreciation of their attendance. Tell them that you value their time and prove it by ending a little early, or using a show of hands to skip a certain point if they already know it or have experience with it. Showing that you respect what they know is always a plus. Thank them sincerely when you are finished and give them the opportunity to reach you later with questions that they just can't stay and ask right now.

IN SHORT

- Consider your audience: how much they know, age, how many other presentations they will be attending, timing of your presentation
- Look for an activity about 30 minutes in to overcome the meal/coffee break/sugar slump. Get

them in groups, find a reason for them to move, challenge them to solve a puzzle, or throw out some trivia questions.

- Show that you appreciate their being there and that you value their time.

CHAPTER 3

Tip 3: Biting the Bullets

Your slides should never be your script.

I really mean it.

Every word you say should not be written on your slides—for a couple of reasons.

First, your audience reads faster than you speak. They will choose to read first and then simply wait for you to catch up and turn to the next slide. If you wanted them to sit and read, you could have printed out the presentation and handed it to them.

For example, if you are going to talk about three ways to improve your website, don't list all three ways and the explanations for each on your slide. **Use one-word hooks, or, even better, a visual.**

Using the example above, let's say that one way to improve a website is to have an interesting *About* page and that a successful *About* page has three components: a photo, a statement of purpose (why you felt it necessary to create the website), and some personal information that makes you interesting to the reader.

Instead of listing those three elements, why not have three visuals on your slide that you can talk about: a photograph frame, a big question mark, and a diary. Your visual learners will love you because they will be able to attach what you say to each of the symbols you've put on the screen. Aural learners will like it, too, because you're only asking them to listen rather than write, read, and listen at the same time. Your other learners will write the words down instead of the pictures anyway, and all will be good.

After you've explained the three necessary elements for a successful *About* page, **back up your theory with examples**. Use views of successful *About* pages or provide your audience with a list of links that they can check on their own later.

You are supposed to be the expert. They came to listen to you. Use the slides to keep their attention on you. This isn't a webinar. You are actually there--in 3D--and your audience wants to connect with you.

IN SHORT

- Your slides should never be your script.
- Use visuals instead of bullet points.
- Use examples.
- Remember, that they came to see and hear you.

CHAPTER 4

Tip 4: Fonts & Color

Here's how to apply the KISS principle to this component of your slides.

1. Use sans serif fonts.

They're easier to read from a distance or on a screen. The font for this book is Times New Roman, but on your e-reader you can choose whatever font is easier for you read. For presentations stick to something clean such as Arial or Calibri. You can see that the spacing and size are quite different for the two of them even though they are both font size 12.

2. Size matters.

The larger the font, the easier the slides are to read. Slides filled with lines of small dense text are an immediate turn off for your audience. Seriously, they won't even bother trying to read them. Keep the font large and simple, and **don't use FULL CAPS**, as they are hard to read at a distance, too.

PowerPoint® offers a large variety of design templates for you to use, but not all of them are going to be easy on your audience's eyes. Extra options, like VisualBee® have even more to choose from. As a rule, **avoid dark backgrounds** and avoid backgrounds that incorporate monochrome patterns.

Always try out your slides in a darkened room ahead of your presentation. Also, check them out in a lit room, too. On the day of the presentation, you might not be able to turn the lights down to the level you want in your presentation room. You might as well be prepared.

4. Colors

If you need to incorporate your company's colors, you can probably find the combination you need under the colors' drop down and use those colors in the borders of your slides only.

For example, if orange, black and white are your company colours, never use the orange for any words on the slides. It's not a good colour at a distance. But the color can be included in a banner across the bottom or along the slide, where you can also add a small version of your company logo.

Bright red or bright blue words on a black background can actually flare and look like they are moving when they are viewed on a screen. Very unnerving, especially if you haven't had that first—or second--cup of coffee. Remember that just because it looks good on your laptop screen, doesn't mean that it will look equally as good for your audience.

Good old black print on a white background is really just fine. Remember the slides aren't what are on show here; it's you and your message. What do you really want your audience to remember at the end of the day? If you make it easy for your audience to access the content, you are doing your job.

5. Italics or Not—Not!

For clean readable text, **avoid slanted fonts or the ones that look like handwriting**. There are lots of other ways to emphasize your text with bolding or highlighting.

Consider that, if you want certain words or phrases to stand out from all the other words, the other words might not have to be there in the first place.

For example, if the information on your slide looks like this—

THINGS TO DO BEFORE WRITING AN ESSAY

First, you need to **brainstorm ideas.**
Second, you need to **choose a topic** and **ask questions** about it.
Third, you need to go online or to the library to **find research resources**.
Fourth, you need to **draft an outline**.

it should probably look like this—

BEFORE WRITING AN ESSAY

1. Brainstorm ideas
2. Narrow the topic
3. Ask questions
4. Find research resources
5. Draft an outline.

While you are speaking, you can fill in the details about how to do all the items from 1 to 5. You can link the list items to examples, or get the audience involved by giving them a topic and asking them to give you their techniques for brainstorming, choosing a topic, etc.

IN SHORT

- Use sans serif fonts.
- Size matters.
- Keep the background clean.
- Colors are important
- No italics

CHAPTER 5

Tip 5: Sound & Action

You can **use both for emphasis,** *once in a while,* **BUT** *not on every slide, please.* When I first introduce PowerPoint® to my classes, the first thing I let them do is play with all the sound and animation tricks. The final results are lots of fun to watch and listen to, but a serious business presentation they are not.

Having your talking points appear on your slide as you make them or after you've made them for emphasis, works fine as a technique, but forget having them slide in and do a little dance every time, or shake, or swoop in with a big swishing noise. They're words not acrobats, and your audience will get tired of the tricks very quickly.

IN SHORT

- Use sound and action rarely.
- Have talking points appear after you've made the point. Treat them as end punctuation to what you are talking about.

CHAPTER 6

Tip 6: The Handout

Handouts are easy. PowerPoint provides a template for handouts of various configurations under the print function.

Not everyone takes notes the same way. The standard PowerPoint® handout lists three slides down the left side of the page and on the right are three groups of blank lines to use for writing notes. That style of note-taking appeals to many people, but there are others who need a little more space.

Take the same miniatures of your slides and centre them on the page with lots of empty white space around them. People like me are more spatial note takers. We like to draw arrows and write on the diagonal, circle things and create a final product that looks like a real mess to the linear note takers, but makes perfect sense to us.

Actually, we do the same thing even if you offer us lines to write on, but we appreciate the option.

It doesn't hurt to have a version of the handout that is in a larger font, perhaps only two slides to a page.

Not everyone has vision that switches well from looking at your slide to looking at the page. The larger print on the page will be more easily accessible to those who have some vision challenges in a dimly lit room.

Don't forget to **offer a follow up email** to those who are interested, so that any live links in your Power-Point® can be available to them along with links to any other background information that might interest your audience. It's a great way to collect email addresses for your mailing list, and develop a ready audience for your next presentation.

IN SHORT

- Use the PowerPoint® handout template for linear thinkers.
- Create a handout for the spatial types.
- Create a handout in larger font for poorly lit rooms and attendees with vision challenges.
- Consider offering an email option

CHAPTER 7

Tip 7: Charts & Tables

Charts and tables can be a presenter's worst nightmare. First, you need to make the image large enough to be seen at the back of the room. If you are using a screen shot for your chart, how clear is it? Does enlarging make everything a bit out of focus? On the handout, will the image be too small to make any sense, especially if it's only printed in black and white?

If you want to discuss a particular, detailed image, print it in colour on paper and hand it out, so that it's large enough for people to read and refer to as you talk about the one you have projected on the screen.

Avoid overlaying data in various colours to show changes over time. It looks nice on your computer screen, but to an audience it can be confusing. Consider using handouts for this information, too.

I can't even think of this topic without immediately picturing the following video. If you do nothing else in this book, watch Don McMillan's hilarious *Life After Death By Powerpoint*:

https://www.youtube.com/watch?v=MjcO2ExtHso

There's a longer version available on YouTube as well. Enjoy.

IN SHORT

- Consider distributing a colour hard copy.
- Avoid overlaying a lot of data.
- **Watch the video**.

CHAPTER 8

Tip 8: The Singer not the Song

After the Starship Enterprise's course was locked in, Captain Jean Luc Picard's instructions consisted of one word, **engage**. That's your job—to engage your audience. Here are some tips to make sure that you do just that.

Face Front

The audience wants to see your face. Turning your back on them to read the content of your slide sends the wrong message. It says that you lack confidence, and that you didn't prepare well enough to know what you are supposed to say without reading it from the screen. That's not to say that you have to have everything memorized, but the notes you speak from should be in your hand or on the podium, not on the screen.

Eye contact

This can be hard to do, but it's easy to fake. If you are in a large room, you can simply look at the tops of people's heads. The people you are looking at will assume you are looking at the person behind them and the ones behind will think you are looking at the person in front of them. The rest of the audience will think, "What great eye contact!" Well, maybe not, but they will see you as confident enough to connect with an audience in stead of looking up into space or staring at the exit sign on the back wall.

Your Voice

If I suggest that you tape yourself as you practise your presentation, you will tell me that you hate your voice on tape. Me, too. In fact, we all do. The voice we hear is from the inside of our head, not the voice others hear on the outside. I, frankly, think I sound like Minnie Mouse, but that's another story.

The backbone of good speaking is good breathing. Every day you should practise breathing from your diaphragm. A voice that is fully supported sounds like it's in control and calm. If you are only breathing from the top half of your lungs, you will run out of breath a lot and sound as if you are anxious or nervous. When you listen to your voice, also listen for the breathing.

If you are wearing a mic for your presentation, it will pick up everything. Listen to some television commentators. Sometimes the mics pick up every inhale, and the commentators sound as if they are gasping for air. (Some interviewers on the Golf Channel come to mind, and it's also common among many guests on Sunday morning political interview shows.) Listen for that sound when you are speaking. Slow down and breathe quietly to avoid that gasp noise after every sentence.

Even if you don't like the *sound* of your voice, there are things that you need to pay attention to that will improve your chances of getting your message across.

Pace

If you rush, people will miss what you are saying. If they miss the content too often, they'll turn off entirely. When you try to slow down, you may think you are speaking glacially slowly. It really isn't the case. Making sure that each word is clear can take a little practice, but it's worth it. If you are using vocabulary that is new to your audience, make sure that you take your time to pronounce it clearly and that it turns up on the screen or on your handout, so that people don't get distracted trying to figure out what you are saying.

Pitch

If you think that your voice sounds too high, you may be right. Try pitching it a little lower. Lower voices convey more authority than high ones, and concentrating on lowering the tone of your voice a bit will also help you slow down. When you listen to your voice, also make sure that you have variety in your pitch and your volume. If everything you say stays all on the same note, the monotonous sound will be a sleeper for your audience.

Rise and Fail

If you want your audience to have confidence in you, don't sound as if every statement you make is a question. Many people have a tendency to raise their voices at the end of every sentence. They sound as if they are always asking a question. They also sound insecure and uncertain. Watch for this one, as it can undermine the confidence you want people to have in you and your message.

For a few more tips, here's a link to a great article by Gina Barnett, an experienced TED talk speaker coach: http://blog.ted.com/a-ted-speaker-coach-shares-11-tips-for-right-before-you-go-on-stage/

IN SHORT

- Face your audience
- Make eye contact
- Breathe from your diaphragm
- Speak slowly and clearly
- Pitch your voice lower for credibility
- Vary the pitch of your voice for emphasis
- Stop making every statement sound like a question

CHAPTER 9

Tip 9: Be Prepared

Stuff happens. Power cables break down. Projector bulbs burn out and there isn't a replacement. The venue's WiFi is unreliable or simply disappears. You can't get the darkness level you want in the room for your presentation, and now the room is so bright that people can't see the slides or so dark that they can't see to write notes.

Whatever you do, **don't spend a lot of time apologizing** for this. Everyone has been in situations where things have happened that are beyond his or her control. Today is your turn. Make a joke. Keep it light. Stay calm. There should be a hitchhiker's guide to presentations that also says in nice friendly letters, *Don't Panic.* Remember your audience is on your side. They want to learn what you are going to tell them. They want you to be a success, so they will meet you more than half way when things go wrong.

Here are some things you might consider as back up:

- If the room is too dark, see if you can open a door or two, preferably near the back of the room. Even a little light can make a big difference to people's comfort level. Room lights are often connected in banks, so play with them, always lighting the back of the room first, so that the slides are visible.
- If you can open a door that shines light on you but isn't too bright to wash out your images, then go for that, too. A poorly lit room means that your face might not be very visible. This means that your voice needs to be louder and clearer. (People hear better when they can see your face.) If people are seated around tables, walk the room a bit as you talk. You should have a hand remote that will control the slides from anywhere.
- Always have an easel, paper and markers on hand. Sometimes venues will provide these for you, but if they don't, it might be worth investing in them for yourself. If for some reason, you can't project your slides or they are barely visible because of a bright room, use the paper to write down your keywords or slide titles as you talk. The movement and writing gives people something to watch.
- If there are too many people for the expense of printing the typical PowerPoint® slide handout, which might be two or three pages,

consider making up a page that has just your slide topics listed. The audience can scribble on that while you speak. Have this prepared ahead of time. If you need it because of equipment breakdowns, your venue should be able to make copies for you quickly.

- Bring your own water. If you like your water cold, bring it in a cooler and consider using an insulated cup or put the water bottle in one of those sleeves that you put on beer and pop tins in the summer. You don't want to have to worry about your hands or anything else getting dripped on from the condensation.

- If the WiFi isn't working, don't apologize. It's not your fault. This is a good time to offer to collect email addresses, so you can send along the links later. Or send your audience members to your website where you will set up a link to your slides and the live links they need. Actually, you should probably have this set up before the presentation.

CHAPTER 10

Step 10: Proofread – Errors look worse in 30 font

Proofread your slides. If you think it's embarrassing to find a typo in an email to a coworker after you've hit send, imagine what a mistake looks like in 30 font to a group of people whose trust or business you are working to keep or earn.

Some proofreading tips:

- If possible, put the project away for a few days before you proofread. You're less likely to catch errors if the material is fresh in your brain because you'll be seeing what you think you wrote, not what you actually wrote.
- Print out your slides. Words look different on the page than they do on a screen. You can spot errors more easily.
- Read your slides in reverse order. Start at your last slide and work back to the beginning. In fact read your individual slides from the bottom up. Our brains are very good at

putting words where we expect them to be when they aren't really there at all.

- Use your finger to follow under the words as you are reading. This helps you slow down and actually look at the words.
- If you are using anyone's name or title of his or her book or company name or work title, double check that these are absolutely correct. Even the name Smith can be spelled more than one way.
- Let someone else have a look at it. Sometimes a fresh pair of eyes will see things that you don't.

A QUICK GUIDE TO BETTER TELEPHONE SKILLS

Introduction

This book is **your quick guide to telephone skills,** or as I originally called it—the lost art of answering the telephone. In five short lessons, you'll have the skills you need to be the best ambassador you can be for your own company or for your employer's through your ability to communicate over the phone.

CHAPTER 1

Your Job as Ambassador

People everywhere talk. People everywhere use the phone. What's the big deal? There's nothing special about talking on the phone.

Well, there is when your livelihood or your employer's depends on the impression you make on customers while talking to them on the phone.

At one time or another, I'm sure that you've had a bad experience with a phone call. You've had to cope with someone's incoherent voice mail message, replaying it several times before you can finally get the person's name and phone number. Or, you've finally gone through all the key-pressing instructions to reach a real person, and you feel like you are interrupting their day.

Using the phone for business, like writing for business, has two purposes:

    3. to make your company look good

    4. to make you look good

In ancient times, such as those when I first went to work in an office, companies had humans answering their phones. And, as a busy temp worker, I often worked for companies that had clients calling from my own country and from around the world.

I was the first voice that callers heard. I was the voice of the company. If I didn't do my job well, the company looked bad. If someone was calling with a complaint, my job was to make sure that they weren't angrier by the time they finally got through to the person who could handle their problem. If the callers didn't know whom they should speak to, my job was to direct them correctly and smoothly. If the person they wanted to speak to was busy, I took a message.

Those days are gone. Many companies have opted for automated phone answering, but that doesn't mean that you're off the hook. Have you called your own voice mail to see what it sounds like? Is there a lot of background noise? Can you hear a smile in your voice, or do you sound uncomfortable or abrupt. Are your words clear? Have you left enough time for someone to write down the other contact number you offer them? Do you repeat important information? As an ambassador for yourself and your company, how do you sound? If you are a manager, have you checked the voicemail messages of your employees? How do they sound to you? How might they sound to a client?

Are you and your company putting your best voice forward? When people say that word of mouth advertising is the most valuable, they're right. People tell their friends about companies or people they liked dealing with, not because the product was brilliant but because the service was—and the service starts with that first call, when they phone to see if you have a product in stock or when you are open. You may figure that you have that covered because many of those questions are all answered by a machine now.

Consider how annoying it is to call a company to see if they have a certain item in stock and then have to wait through the spiel about the stores hours, and how to find the website, and where your store is located. The caller doesn't want any of that information, and you've just wasted his or her time--not a crowd-pleaser. Offer that information as an option that they can access by pressing a certain number. Telling people what they don't want to know is not service. Getting them to the information they need as soon as possible *is*.

Nothing annoys me more than to phone a company and have the voice on the other end tell me the company's website address. Believe me, if the website had the answer I was looking for, I wouldn't be phoning. I always feel that no one at the company really wants to talk to me, and is trying to avoid the call by sending me somewhere else. It makes me wary about how I will be treated when I do reach a person, since the message seems to be that person-to-person contact is not welcome.

Most people shop online, so you don't have to worry about phone service if you have a good web-

site. *And if you believe that, you're missing out on an opportunity to keep a customer for life.* People shop online, but they do a lot of comparison shopping first. If potential customers decide to call you for information, that's a bonus opportunity for you to make an impression that will stay with them and be passed along to their friends. People appreciate the feeling of being valued. Regular unsolicited emails to "Our Valued Customer Joe" or your mission statement on your website won't come close to creating that *we-think-you're-important feeling* that a friendly, interested voice on the phone can convey.

CHAPTER 2

Saying Hello

The most important gift you can give your caller is your complete attention, so you need to demonstrate that right from the beginning of the call. Human hearing is fine-tuned to the nuances of a person's voice. You know from your own experience that you can hear when someone is not really paying attention just by the way their voice sounds. Hearing keyboard clicks in the background as someone finishes an email while distractedly answering your call doesn't make you feel important. You're clearly just an interruption, and if you are calling with a problem, feeling like that won't make you feel positive about what might happen next.

The first rule for making your caller feel important is **take your time.** Yes, I know you're busy, but so are your callers. They know their hourly rate, too, and they know how much this phone call is costing them out of their billable hours. Respect that.

Look away from your computer screen and actually **take a breath** before you answer the phone. There's no bonus for picking up on the first ring.

Smile when you greet the caller. If you are smiling, the caller can hear it. It's a very welcoming sound, and much appreciated after what might have been a long wait to canned music that isn't remotely to the caller's taste.

Greeting the caller with just your name isn't enough. The caller needs a couple of words to get into listening gear, so say *good morning* or *good afternoon* before adding, *Heather Wright speaking*. Your caller is probably expecting a machine so give him or her time to get over the shock of actually being able to talk to a human. This extra little moment gets you focused, too.

Always have pen/pencil and paper on hand to take notes. Even if, in order to answer the question, you will need to check something on your computer, it doesn't hurt to have paper nearby to take a note or two. You might have to forward information to someone else after the call is over. or you might promise your caller that you are going to do something by a certain time after the call is over. Write it down and you won't forget.

If you have to put the caller on hold, **never say *just a minute* or "*just*" *anything***. Using the word *just* makes you sound impatient. It's better to say. *Thanks, Ms. Smith. I have to put your call on hold while I look that up. Please stay on the line, and I'll be back to you as quickly as possible.*

IN SHORT

- Take your time.
- Smile when you greet the caller.
- Greeting the caller with just your name isn't enough.
- Always have pen/pencil and paper on hand to take notes.
- Never say *just a minute* or *just a sec.*

CHAPTER 3

Leaving A Voice Mail Message

Before making your call consider what you will say if you get directed to voice mail instead of reaching the person that you hope to speak to. **You need to know the time you are calling,** when and how you can be reached for the person to call back, and be able to **summarize your message in about two sentences.**

Here's the pattern for an effective voice message.

Hi Henry. It's Heather Wright calling at 10 AM on Wednesday the 15th. I'm phoning to ask if you have another contact person I can approach for the article you've asked me to write for the company blog. Chris, the contact you gave me, is away on vacation and won't be back until after the article is due. Please give me a call at 555-123-4567. (Pause) Heather Wright 555-123-4567.

Tell the caller your name up front, but still repeat your name at the end of the message. Henry might not have heard my name correctly at the beginning of the message. Someone could have interrupted him or people could be talking in the background. He might not have a pen in his hand to write down my number the first time. When I repeat my name and number at the end, I repeat it more slowly--**at writing speed**, so Henry doesn't have to replay the message to get the number right.

If Henry's using his smartphone, of course, he can save your number right away, but it doesn't hurt to make sure. If his smartphone turns voice mail into email or text messages, it's even more important to speak slowly and clearly. You never know what your words will *look* like compared to what they *sound* like.

The time and date of your call are important, too. If Henry doesn't pick up his messages for a few days, he can prioritize his return calls better if he knows when his callers contacted him or when a response is time sensitive.

IN SHORT

- Plan your message
- Begin with your name and time
- Keep the message short and to the point.
- End with how to contact you.
- Repeat your name and phone number in "writing speed" at the end of your message.

CHAPTER 4

The Message Others Hear

Take a moment to **listen to the message your callers hear on your voicemail**. People generally hate recording these messages and get the process over with as quickly as possible. Sometimes those feelings come through loud and clear.

Prepare your script. If you have to record these every day (as some companies expect), make sure you try to approach them with a fresh smile, even though it's the 150th time this year you've said the same words.

Take your time and speak clearly and slowly. (What sounds slow to you sounds just fine to your audience.) If you suggest another person and extension for your caller to contact, make sure that you say that person's name slowly enough for the caller to hear. Your caller will hesitate to call that person, if he or she is afraid to make a mistake pronouncing the person's name—was it Helen or Ellen, or Rich or Mitch. No one wants to feel foolish.

If you do record a message every day, **make sure that your message is updated every day**. There's nothing more confusing than calling someone on Tuesday whose message still thinks it's Friday.

Listen to the cadence of your voice. If you are one of those people who raises the pitch of his or her voice at the end of every sentence, try hard to avoid that in your voicemail message. When your voice goes up at the ends of sentences, it sounds as if you are asking a question—as if you are uncertain or nervous. Practise dropping the pitch of your voice at the end of the sentence to sound more confident and professional. This is a good technique to learn for presentations and job reviews, too.

IN SHORT

- Prepare your script.
- Take your time and speak clearly and slowly
- Make sure that your message is updated every day
- Listen to the cadence of your voice

CHAPTER 5

Answering the Phone for Your Company

If you are the first voice that a caller to your company hears, you have a big responsibility. I know from experience how crazy it can be sitting in your chair. Depending upon the number of lines you have coming in, it can be hard not to feel rushed when lights are flashing for your attention.

Take a deep breath. Ten rings of a phone equal 30 seconds, so if you answer after five or six, the caller hasn't really spent that much time waiting for you to pick up. If the voice the caller hears is pleasant and calm, the number of rings it took to get the phone answered won't matter. If the voice is curt and sounds rushed, the caller will hear that, too, and feel that he or she is an inconvenience rather than someone that you want to welcome to your company. If the caller is already feeling impatient, that voice won't help the mood.

Make sure that you say your company's name clearly and slowly preceded by a "good morning" or "good afternoon." The caller needs a moment to realize that the call has been answered before tuning in. Many companies will have a script for you to follow. Often you will include an offer to help along with the company name: "Good morning, Parkinson Electric. How may I help you?" or "Good morning, Parkinson Electric. Carol speaking. How may I help you?"

Once you figure out what the caller wants, what do you say next?

Let's say that the caller asks to speak to Louise. **If the caller hasn't given you his or her name at the beginning of the call, you need to find it out.** It's very helpful to Louise if she knows who is calling. She might need a moment to find his file, or she might not want to talk to that person at all right now. You need to say to the caller, "May I tell Louise who is calling?" Generally, that will get you a name. Let's say the caller is Bill Mackenzie.

Next, **do not say**, "Thanks, I'll put you right through" unless you are absolutely certain that Louise is at her desk and able to or wants to take the call. Instead say, "Thanks, Mr. Mackenzie, I'll check if she's available" and put him on hold. Then you can buzz Louise and tell her Bill Mackenzie is on the line. If she's happy to talk to him, that's great. Go back to Bill and say, "Thanks for waiting, Mr. Mackenzie. I'll put you right through." If Louise isn't there or can't/won't talk to him, go back to Bill and say, "I'm sorry, Mr. Mackenzie. Louise is on a long call right now, would you like to leave a message on her voicemail?" Then, Bill has the option to leave a message or call back another time. And yes, **the fine art of fibbing is part of the receptionist's job.**

A QUICK GUIDE TO BETTER WRITING & GRAMMAR

Introduction

This book is **your quick guide to better writing and grammar**. The tips in this book will help you develop the strategies you need to find and correct errors that can reflect badly on you as a professional. This book doesn't cover every grammar, punctuation, and writing problem, but it is designed to hit the most common errors that might be holding you back from producing clean, correct writing.

Bad grammar can cost you money. If that alone isn't a motivator, consider this. How can clients trust you with a detailed financial project you are doing on their behalf, when you can't be bothered to pay attention to the details of spelling and grammar?

Or consider this: you are just starting in the workplace and the people you work for or want to work for aren't your generation. They don't communicate in the same way that your friends do via text and in person. If you want to impress employers, get the grammar right.

Employers consider good writing and speaking skills as the *minimum* skills you should have in order to be a competent worker. If your work doesn't meet those standards, then how can you represent their company at a higher level? Their employees are their companies' ambassadors; they want their ambassadors to impress not embarrass.

Yes, checking your work for grammar and spelling errors will take a little extra time, but consider it an investment in your career. As you learn to recognize and correct your errors, you should eventually stop making them in the first place, and you'll get back up to speed again.

Here are four articles that might convince you that spelling and grammar matter:

1. "Spelling and Grammar Matter in Marketing" by Kara Sassone. Kara links to other articles that demonstrate the benefits of good grammar and spelling.
http://blog.hubspot.com/blog/tabid/6307/bid/203 83/Why-Spelling-and-Grammar-Matter-in-Marketing.aspx

2. CEO Kyle Weins explains in the *Harvard Business Review* why he won't hire people with poor grammar skills. https://hbr.org/2012/07/i-wont-hire-people-who-use-poo

3. "Realtor listings: Bad grammar and typos cost agents money, according to U.S. study" by Shari Kulha.
http://news.nationalpost.com/homes/realtor-listings-bad-grammar-and-typos-cost-agents-money-according-to-u-s-study

4. "Bad Grammar Will Lose Your Online Business Money" by Jason Walker.
http://www.searchandmore.co.uk/internet-marketing/bad-grammar-lose-online-business-money/

Other books previously released in this Better Business Communication series cover presentations, emails, telephone skills, and improving your writing and grammar. All are available at your online bookseller.

CHAPTER 1

Tip 1: Avoid Wordiness

No this isn't a grammar or a spelling error, but wordiness will hurt the first impression that your writing makes with your readers. I know that you want to sound courteous and respectful to your reader, but that can translate into wasting the reader's time with a lot of unnecessary words. You may be very polite, but none of that matters if your reader is inwardly screaming, "Get to the point!" You also need to respect your reader's time. Don't waste it; instead, choose the following options.

One word instead of many

It's easy to get carried away with your own words, especially when you are trying to make an impression. Simpler is better and you can still be polite without being wordy. The following is an example of a wordy email message:

Thank you so much for kindly responding to my inquiry so quickly. The committee and I were very pleased to read your response and are very hon-

oured that you have agreed to speak to our managers on the 14th. In response to your request for suggested topics for your speech, we have surveyed our managers who were very happy to reply to our request. Here are the topics that they have suggested. (72 words)

Instead, consider this:

Thanks for getting back to me so quickly. We really appreciate your agreeing to speak to our managers on the 14th. You asked for some possible topics, and my managers suggested the following: (33 words)

Sometimes we get into bad habits and uses stock phrases without realizing that there are less wordy alternatives. Here are some examples of groups of words that can be replaced by just one.

Some groups of words say the same things twice:

Mutual agreement	An agreement, by definition, has to be mutual.
Future prospects	Prospects are always in the future
Advance warning	If a warning isn't in advance, it's not much use.

You get the idea. There are lots of other groups of words that can be replaced by a simpler option.

At this point in time	Now, Today
Make an assumption	Assume
In today's society	Today
Came to a realization	Realized

Here is a link to a comprehensive list of words you can eliminate or change to avoid wordiness in your writing:
http://web.uvic.ca/~gkblank/wordiness.html

Organize

Put your ideas into short paragraphs. When you change topic, make a new paragraph. Nothing looks less appealing to read than one long dense piece of text on a page.

Thanks for getting back to me so quickly. We really appreciate your agreeing to speak to our managers on the 14th. You asked for some possible topics. Here are some that my managers suggested. They wanted you to talk about the latest changes to Product C. They also wanted information about introducing customers to our new website. Could you also tell them about the expansion to the eastern headquarters? Many managers wanted to know if you spotted any new trends at the Waterloo convention you attended. I'll be sending you the full program for the meeting as soon as it is complete. If

you have any questions, please contact me at ext.
234.
Thanks again.

Here's how the message looks now with paragraphs and a bullet list to help organize the information in a way that is accessible by the reader:

Thanks for getting back to me so quickly. We really appreciate your agreeing to speak to our managers on the 14th.

You asked for some possible topics. Here are some that my managers suggested:

1) The latest changes to product C

2) Strategies for introducing customers to the new website

3) An update on the expansion of the eastern headquarters

4) Any new trends that you spotted at the Waterloo convention

I'll be sending you the full program for the meeting as soon as it is complete. If you have any questions, please contact me at ext. 234.

Thanks again.

Heather

IN SHORT

- Use one word instead of many.
- Organize ideas into short paragraphs
- Use bullet point lists

CHAPTER 2

Tip 2: Use Bullet Point Lists
to Organize Data

Lists hidden in paragraphs look like long unbroken clumps of words on the screen and are not reader-friendly. Here's an example of a wordy paragraph from the previous chapter:

You asked for some possible topics. Here are some that my managers suggested. They wanted you to talk about the latest changes to Product C. They also wanted information about introducing customers to our new website. Could you also tell them about the expansion to the eastern headquarters? Many managers wanted to know if you spotted any new trends at the Waterloo convention you attended.

The above paragraph is wordy and the ideas in it can be explained more clearly using bullet points, as below:

You asked for some possible topics and my managers suggested the following:

- *The latest changes to product C*
- *Strategies for introducing customers to the new website*
- *An update on the expansion of the eastern headquarters*
- *Any new trends that you spotted at the Waterloo convention*

Lists are a very efficient way to present information, but they need to have a very specific format. Use bullets when listing a series of items. Use numbers when listing a set of steps that have to be followed in order or to prioritize the list by ranking the information in order.

Rules for Bullet Lists

Lists are a very efficient way to present information in your email, but they need to have a very specific format. Use bullets when listing a series of items. Use numbers when listing a set of steps that have to be followed in order or to prioritize the list by ranking the information in order.

Rules for the Lead In

If the lead-in that precedes the list is a complete sentence, you end it with a colon.

Examples

The following are the four points I'd like you to consider:

Here are the 5 steps you need to follow:

Please answer the following questions:

The material required includes the following:

If the lead-in is not a complete sentence, that means that the material following the lead-in is completing the sentence; therefore, the lead-in has no punctuation after it.

Examples

The four steps require to complete this project are

It's important to remember that

I'd appreciate your input on

Rules for Punctuation

Here are a couple of examples that show how the rest of the list is punctuated.

Example 1

Please complete the following and return them to me by Friday:

- Status Form 1303
- Standard Release 12
- Personnel Questionnaire
- Tax Form C35689

Because the list above follows a complete sentence, there is no end punctuation after the items in the list

Example 2

In order to be ready for the meeting, you will need to

- review the Benson contract,
- bring tax information relating to the Morris partnership, and
- review the Hendley incorporation documents.

Note that in example 2, the list is punctuated as if it were written out as one long sentence with commas after the items in the list. If it were written out as a sentence, it would look like the following:

In order to be ready for the meeting, you will need to review the Benson contract, bring tax information relating to the Morris partnership, and review the Hendley incorporation documents.

Rules for the contents

All of the items in the list need to follow the same pattern. In Example 2, all of the items in the list are nouns/things. In Example 2, every point begins with a verb/action: review, bring, review.

Here's an example of a list in which the items don't follow the same pattern.

On Friday morning
- Bring your laptop
- Go to meeting room B
- You'll need a 2G memory stick.

In the above example, the first two items begin with verbs (bring, go) and the third item is a sentence starting with the pronoun, you. Since all the items in the list need to match, the third item also needs to start with a verb.

On Monday morning
- bring your laptop,
- go to meeting room B,
- bring an empty 2G memory stick.

Here are two more before and after examples. When you write your lists correctly, it's called parallel construction.

When winter comes, we love to
- ski
- make snowmen
- skate in the park
- making snow angels at Grandma's house.

When winter comes, we love to

- ski,
- make snowmen,
- skate in the park,
- make snow angels at Grandma's house.

Here are some steps you need to complete in order to write a report:
- Brainstorm ideas
- Find research sources
- Draft an outline
- Writing the first draft comes next

Here are some steps you need to complete in order to write a report:
- Brainstorm ideas
- Find research sources
- Draft an outline
- Write the first draft

IN SHORT

- If the lead-in is a complete sentence, it is followed by a colon.
- The items in a list preceded by a colon begin with a capital letter. If they are single words or phrases, they need no end punctuation. If

they are short sentences, each sentence needs a period at the end.
- If the lead-in is not a complete sentence, no punctuation is required.
- The items in a list following an incomplete sentence do not begin with a capital letter and are followed by commas with a period at the end—as if you were writing it out as one long sentence.
- All items in the list need to follow the same format—parallel construction.

CHAPTER 3

Tip 3: Easily Confused Words

The words below when used incorrectly are rarely caught by spell checking programs.

Than/then
These two words have very different purposes. *Than* is used to compare: He has more money *than* I have. *Then* is used to indicate time. We went to the bank; *then* we went to the restaurant. One way to remember the difference is that there is an "a" in compare (than/compare) and an "e" in time (then/time).

A lot/Allot
A lot is never one word. *Allot* means to portion out: Because she had *a lot* of candy, she was able to *allot* two candy bars to each of the children.

Their/there/they're

Their is a possessive pronoun. They drove *their* old van to the east coast. *Their* has the words *he* and *I* in it—two people—so it relates to two or more people owning something.

There indicates a place. We left the van over *there*. *There* also has the word *here* in it—another place, just closer.

They're is a contraction for "they are." In contractions, apostrophes usually mean that letters are left out. An exception would be *won't*, but others follow the rule: cannot – *can't*; would not – *wouldn't*. Remembering that will stop you from writing *would'nt* because the apostrophe in the misspelled word isn't replacing anything.

To/too/two

Two is the number 2.

Too means as well. He went to the game, *too*. Generally, "too" is set off from the rest of the sentence with a comma. Sometimes *too* means *extra* and is usually followed by another word that describes the topic: I ate *too* much ice cream. (much describes how much ice cream was eaten.) Yesterday was *too* hot (hot describes the day) She was too tired to go to the party. (tired describes the woman) This is a little easier to remember because there's an

extra *o* in *too* to go with the extra ice cream, the extra heat, the extra feeling of being tired.

To has one purpose—to introduce something—a noun phrase or a verb. I went *to* the store. We were not required *to* register until Thursday morning.

Who's/Whose

Who's is the contraction of who is. The apostrophe replaces the missing "I" in "is".

Whose is the possessive pronoun. Like all possessive pronouns it shows ownership without using an apostrophe: hers, theirs, its, his, yours.

It's/Its

It's is the contraction for it is. The apostrophe replaces the "i" in "is."

Its is the possessive pronoun.

It's time for the dog to have *its* bath.

Affect/Effect

Affect is the action and is a verb. (A for affect, A for action). After three days of rain, the gloomy weather *affected* our mood. The weather is acting on the people's moods.

Effect is the end product and is a noun. (E for effect. E for end product.) The *effect* of the gloomy weather was to make everyone grumpy. The end product/result of the gloomy weather was everyone's gloomy mood.

Loose/Lose

Loose means that something is not tight. When you *lose* something, it is lost. A good way to remember how to spell the latter is to lose an "o" when you spell lose.

Accept/Except

Accept means receive. Peter *accepted* (received) the award from the president.

Except can be replaced with the word *excluding*. We were all ready to leave *except* (excluding) Bill who was looking for his gloves. Peter can eat anything *except* (excluding) gluten. Since *except* begins with the same three letters as *exclude*, it's easy to remember the difference.

IN SHORT

- Don't rely on a spellchecker to get these words right.
- When in doubt, use a dictionary or use the thesaurus option on your word processing program. In Word, the thesaurus option can be found under the Review tab. Either op-

tion will tell you whether you've chosen the correct word.

CHAPTER 4

Tip 4: Paragraphing

Nothing is as discouraging to a reader as a long, solid chunk of writing on the page. If you've written a really long paragraph, chances are that it's not one paragraph. Look for places to break it up into smaller chunks. In Chapter 2, we looked at the option of using bullet lists to break up long paragraphs. Another way to break up a long piece of unbroken text, is to look for places when the topic changes or the when time changes.

Email messages are usually fairly short. It's okay to have one-sentence paragraphs.

Here's an example **before revision**.

Dear Bill, Thanks for asking for my input into the proposed policy changes. I agree that the new policy has many advantages that will be evident to our employees, but I think that one element needs to be explained further. I think it's important that people know the reasons for the new policy, not simply to be handed the new policy and be expected to implement it. Change can be challenging for many, and this policy does represent a significant change. Understanding the reasons for the change helps employees adapt and accept new policies more readily. This blog post by work-change expert, John Smith, explains what I mean more clearly: http://urlofexpert. I would appreciate the opportunity to speak further with you about the launch of this new policy and strategies to make it more accessible to our employees. Please give me a call today or tomorrow, so that we can set up a time to get together soon.

Best regards,
Heather Wright
Vice-President Administration

Here's the **revised version**:

Dear Bill,

Thanks for asking for my input into the proposed policy changes. I agree that the new policy has many advantages that will be evident to our employees, but I think that one key element needs to be explained further. (**topic change** - new topic starts in next paragraph where the writer adds more details about the key element)

I think it's important that people know the reasons for the new policy, not simply to be handed the new policy and be expected to implement it.

Change can be challenging for many, and this policy does represent a significant change. Understanding the reasons for the change helps employees adapt and accept new policies more readily. This blog post by work-change expert, John Smith, explains what I mean more clearly: www.urlofexpert. (**time change** - next paragraph is looking forward to next steps)

I would appreciate the opportunity to speak further with you about the launch of this new policy and strategies to make it more accessible to our employees. Please give me a call today or tomorrow, so that we can set up a time to get together soon.

Best regards,
Heather Wright
Vice-President Administration

IN SHORT

- Look for changes in time or topic to find ways to break long paragraphs into shorter ones.
- In emails, it's okay to have one-sentence paragraphs.

CHAPTER 5

Tip 5: Run-On Sentences
or
What a Comma Can't Do

Run-on sentences are sentences that are really two or three sentences all strung together without proper punctuation.

Example: It's important for us all to attend the meeting on Saturday morning, we have to discuss the gift for the departing president, we also need to talk about the summer barbeque.

The person writing the sentence above knew that there were three different thoughts included in that long sentence and thought that a comma would be fine to divide the thoughts from each other. WRONG. Commas are the busiest of the punctuation marks and can do many things (see the next chapter), but the one thing they cannot do is hold two complete sentences together all by themselves.

Here are some correct options for punctuating the above group of sentences.

Use periods to make each sentence correct.
It's important for us all to attend the meeting on Saturday morning. We have to discuss the gift for the departing president. We also need to talk about the summer barbeque.

Use a semi-colon to join two sentences.
Semi-colons are used to connect two complete sentences when the second sentence adds more information to the first.

It's important for us all to attend the meeting on Saturday morning. We have to discuss the gift for the departing president; we also need to talk about the summer barbeque.

Use a comma and one of the FANBOYS.
Commas can join two complete sentences, BUT only when they are partnered with one of the following conjunctions: **f**or, **a**nd, **n**or, **b**ut, **o**r, **y**et, **s**o. **FANBOYS** for short.

*It's important for us all to attend the meeting on Saturday morning. We have to discuss the gift for the departing president, **and** we also need to talk about the summer barbeque.*

Eliminate repeated words and combine the sentences into a shorter sentence.

The new sentence below eliminated the repeated words "we have to" and "we also need to".

It's important for us all to attend the meeting on Saturday morning to discuss the gift for the departing president and talk about the summer barbeque.

IN SHORT

- Commas can't connect two complete sentences.
- Break run-on sentences into separate complete sentences.
- Connect the sentences with a semi-colon.
- Connect the sentences with a comma followed by one of the **FANBOYS.**
- Combine the sentences by eliminating repeated words

CHAPTER 6

Tip 6: Commas–What They Can Do

Commas are everywhere, but they're not always in the right place. One of the rules for using commas that people often use is to stick one in wherever they take a breath. If that were the case, I would have put a comma in the previous sentence in front of the word *is*. And that would have been wrong. You can never use a comma to separate the subject of a sentence from its verb. The sentence begins with a very long group of words (*One of the rules for using commas that people often use*), but it is also the subject of the sentence, and it can't be separated from the verb *is* with a comma. Uh uh. No. Never.

Here are some places where you should use commas.

Dates

Use commas to separate the date from the year or the month from the year.

September 23, 2016
The comma is not needed when the date is not indicated: September 2016

Place names
In addresses, use commas to separate various parts of the address. There are no commas after the street number.
Toronto, Ontario, Canada or London, England
123 Anywhere Street, Yourtown, Province/State

After introductory words, clauses or phrases.
Groups of words that introduce a sentence are separated from the sentence by a comma.
After several weeks of practice, Jim was ready to enjoy the canoe trip.
Unless we hear from you by January 3, 2016, your account will be frozen.
On Tuesday, we were able to finalize the contract.
I stayed home to study on Monday night. However, my friends went out for pizza and a movie.
(These two sentences can be combined into one sentence using a semi-colon: I stayed home to study on Monday night; however, my friends went out for pizza and a movie.)

Before quotations
Use a comma to introduce a quotation.
Hannah said, "I would like to call the meeting to order."
The president remarked, "That was an excellent presentation."

To indicate non-essential information or an interruption
Sometimes we add information in a sentence, but the sentence makes perfect sense without it. In that case, you put commas around the non-essential information. Here are some examples:
I love to try different flavors of ice cream. Jim, as always, chose vanilla.
Every Saturday, though I missed last week, I go to the farmers' market.
If the information is essential to the meaning of the sentence, then it needs no commas.
Athletes who warm up before strenuous activity suffer fewer injuries.
The procedures that are listed in the enclosed document replace section 5 of the contract.
It's important to know which athletes suffer fewer injuries and which procedures replace section 5 in the contract so no commas separate that information from the rest of the sentence.

If the added piece of information or interrupting statement comes after one of the FANBOYS, it doesn't need a comma in front of it.

I was thrilled to receive the award, and as expected, I burst into tears when I thought of my family's support.

Too is a word that is often set apart from the rest of the sentence if it interrupts a statement or appears at the end.

Notice, *too,* that the CEO travelled three times to Vancouver to deal with the problem.

In this sentence commas set apart the word *too* from the rest of the sentence. Use a comma in front of the words *too, also,* and others at the ends of sentences, as well. I like chocolate ice cream, but I like other flavors, *too.*

In a list

When you have three or more adjectives describing a noun, they need to be separated by commas. There is no comma required to separate the final adjective from the word *and* though sometimes it is necessary in order for the sentence to make sense.

It was a dark, stormy and rainy night.

If you wrote that *it was a very dark, stormy and rainy night*, you don't put a comma between *very* and *dark* because the word *very* is an adverb and is never separated from the word it is describing by a comma. Other examples of adverbs include *really, terribly, honestly, literally,* etc. Lots of adverbs end in *ly,* and lots of times, sentences work just fine without them.

The following examples show different lists with the items separated by commas:

Jim ran to the car, tried to open the door, and remembered that he'd forgotten his keys.

When you meet someone new, remember to stand tall, make eye contact, and repeat his or her name right away.

If the items in your list have commas included in them, then you need to use semi-colons to separate the different items in the list.

When preparing for a long trip, it's important to pack all your prescription drugs; a first aid kit that includes bandages, antibacterial ointment, and antiseptic; a list of emergency contacts; and extra batteries and chargers for your electronics.

Here's an example of a list that shows the necessity of using the extra comma in front of *and.*

When Jim accepted his Oscar, *he thanked his parents, Kanye West and Meryl Streep.*

If the sentence above is left the way it is, it reads as if Jim's parents are Kanye West and Meryl

Streep. To make it clear that Jim is thanking all the people individually, the sentence needs to be punctuated like this:

When Jim accepted his Oscar, *he thanked his parents, Kanye West, and Meryl Streep.*

If there is any doubt about making your meaning clear, use the comma before the *and* in the sentence.

Commas and *That*

Commas aren't necessary when you use *that* in a sentence.

Here are some examples:

Jim said that *Survivor* was his favorite TV show.

The shirt that I bought yesterday matched my jacket perfectly.

When Jim was a child, he dreamed that he would be a doctor when he grew up.

IN SHORT

- To learn a lot more about commas check this link: https://owl.english.purdue.edu/owl/owlprint/607/
- To practise and check your comma knowledge check this link: https://owl.english.purdue.edu/exercises/3/5/15

CHAPTER 7

Tip 7: Fragments

Fragments are bits of sentences that aren't complete but are punctuated as if they were. *Such as this. Such as this* contains no subject and no verb, so it isn't a sentence and can't just sit by itself with a capital letter at the beginning and a period at the end.

See if you can spot the fragments below:

1. Yesterday we went to the shopping mall.
2. We needed to buy groceries plus presents for the twins, Emily and Michael.
3. Because it was their birthday on Sunday.
4. Emily loves anything to do with Dora the Explorer®.
5. Michael likes Lego®.
6. Lots of toy stores with a variety of items on sale.
7. We were happy at the end of the day to have bought everything we needed.
8. Very tired and glad to go home.

Numbers 3, 6, and 8 are fragments. My word processing software only caught number 3 and marked it as a fragment, so don't rely on a green squiggly line to tell you that you've made a mistake.

Number 3 can be fixed by adding it to the sentence above. *We needed to buy groceries plus presents for the twins, Emily and Michael, because it was their birthday on Sunday.*

Number 6 needs a bit more work. It needs a subject (we) and a verb (visited). *We visited lots of toy stores with a variety of items on sale.*

Number 8 has the same problem. It needs a subject (we) and a verb (were). *We were very tired and glad to go home.*

When you are proofreading, read each individual sentence slowly. You will be able to hear when something is missing and be able to make the changes you need to correct the error.

IN SHORT

- Fragments are incomplete sentences. They are missing a verb or a subject or both.
- Word processing software won't catch all of these.
- Proofread slowly to catch the sentences that just don't sound right, and add the verb, subject or both to correct the error.

CHAPTER 8

Tip 8: Where to Capitalize

Getting the capital letters in the right place will make your writing look clean and professional. Throwing a capital letter on a random word to make it look important is just wrong.

For example--

Yesterday I heard from Eric about the progress on the Report he is writing with Phil and Alisha. Each of them has taken control of one aspect of the Report and they have asked Lena to be their Editor when the work is finally finished.

Poet <u>Emily Dickinson</u> loved using capital letters for effect, but they don't work so well in every day business correspondence unless they are required. The nouns *report* and *editor* in the above example don't need capital letters. Also, don't go to the other extreme and ignore them altogether. I received a note one year that looked like this:

i'm so glad that you were able to say yes to our invitation. we are very pleased to know we will have you on board for the day. hope everything is well with you. all the best, etc.... This writer went straight from Emily Dickinson to <u>e.e. cummings</u>!

People's names need capital letters, but the nouns capitalized above (report, editor) don't need capital letters.

Unless you are writing in your native language and it capitalizes all nouns or you are channeling Emily, nouns in English only need a capital letter if they are the name of a city, state, province, country, street, school, historic landmark, body of water, etc. Think geography or maps and think capital letters. Days of the week, months of the year, and holidays require capital letters, too.

Directions (north, south, east, west, etc.) don't require capital letters. If a direction is being used to also describe a political entity, then it will require a capital. The North won the Civil War. The names of the seasons don't need capital letters either.

A person's title gets a capital letter when the person's name follows it or when the title refers to a specific person:

- Prime Minister Cameron
- Reverend Jones
- The President addressed the nation.

However, if you are just talking about the job they are doing then you don't need to capitalize the title:

- It must be challenging to be a president of a large company.
- Jim said he always wanted to be the mayor of our town.

For more information on capitalization rules, check the Purdue OWL site.

IN SHORT

- Capitalize days of the week and months of the year.
- Capitalize names of cities, states, provinces, countries, streets, schools, historic landmarks, bodies of water, etc.
- Do not capitalize seasons or directions.
- Capitalize job titles when followed by a person's name or when the job title refers to a specific person.

CHAPTER 9

Tip 9: Who, Whom, Everyone, Everybody, I, Me

Who/Whom and others

Pronouns replace nouns and they do it in two ways. They can be either the subject or the object in a sentence.

Subject Pronouns	Object Pronouns
I	Me
He	Him
She	Her
They	Them
Who	Whom
It/You	It/You

You use the subject form of the pronoun when it is the subject of the sentence. The object form is used after prepositions or verbs. Examples of prepositions are *with, to, in, into, between, without, among, under, above, over, on,* etc.

I went to the store.—*I* is the subject of the sentence.

He went with *me.*—*Me* comes after the preposition *with* and is the object of the phrase *with me.*

If you have two pronouns together or a noun and a pronoun together and you're not sure whether you are using the pronouns correctly, try the sentence with only one of them and see if it makes sense.

Let's say that your sentence is *Jim and me went to the store.* Leave out the word, *Jim,* and say the sentence without it. You recognize right away that *Me went to the store* is wrong. You would say *I went to the store,* so the correct sentence is *Jim and I went to the store.*

Here's another example. *Him and me are going shopping.* You would never say *Him is going shopping* or *Me is going shopping,* so the correct sentence is *He and I are going shopping.*

Remember those prepositions I mentioned? After a preposition, use the object form of the pronoun.

Henry went with Carol and me.

This secret is just between you and me. For this example, I know that you want to say *you and I,* but that would be incorrect. Using the pronoun *I* might sound more formal or proper (and song writers have been using it forever in order to make the rhyme they need) but *between you and me* really is correct.

And I'm not the only one who thinks so:
https://owl.english.purdue.edu/owl/resource/595/02/

After *than* and *as*

To make sure that you choose the correct pronoun in sentences using **than** or **as**, always make sure to complete the sentence in your head to help you choose the correct pronoun.
Jim is a better singer than I.
Jim is a better singer than I am.
Linda is as good a runner as I.
Linda is as good a runner as I am.
Mike is as skilled as he.
Mike is as skilled as he is.
Helen is a faster runner than she.
Helen is a faster runner than she is.

Everyone/everybody/each/every etc.

The two tricks for the words in this list and others, such as somebody and everyone, is choosing what form of the verb to use after them and what personal pronouns to use.

Here's an example:

Each of the employees want a raise.

Each is treated as a singular subject, so it needs a singular verb. The correct sentence is *Each* of the employees *wants* a raise. When you are faced with words such as anybody, anyone, each, each one, either, everyone, everybody, neither, nobody, no one, somebody, and someone replace them in your mind with the words *he* or *she*. *She wants a raise*. Another method that will help is to block out the words that are in between the subject and the verb. In the example above, ignore the words *of the employees* and then choose your verb: *Each wants a raise*.

IN SHORT

For more tips on using these tricky words and a quiz, check here:
http://www.grammarbook.com/grammar/pronoun.asp

CHAPTER 10

Tip 10: Proofread

Some proofreading tips:

- If possible, put the project away for a few days before you proofread. You're less likely to catch errors if the material is fresh in your brain because you'll be seeing what you're thinking and not what you actually wrote.
- Print out your material. Words look different on the page than they do on a screen. You can spot errors more easily.
- Read your work in reverse order. Start at your last paragraph and work back to the beginning. In fact, reading your work from the bottom up is a great way to catch problems in any project because it makes our brain work a little differently. Our brains are very good at putting words

where we expect them to be when they aren't there at all.

- Use your finger to follow under the words as you are reading. This helps you slow down and actually look at the words.
- If you are using anyone's name or title of his or her book or company name or work title, double check that these are absolutely correct. Even the name Smith can be spelled more than one way.
- Let someone else have a look at it. Sometimes a fresh pair of eyes will see things that you don't.

If you want to delve further into the mechanics of grammar and punctuation and do some self-testing, check out the resources at Purdue OWL.

IN SHORT

- Give the project a rest.
- Read in reverse order
- Follow the words with your finger
- Double check names and titles
- Let someone else check your work.

Last Words

There is no magic bullet for success in your career, but you can bet that making a good impression through your communication skills won't hurt and may just set you above the rest.

Good luck with meeting your business goals. One of my goals is to sell more books. If you found this guide of value, please stop by your online bookseller and leave a review. I appreciate your time and your honest comments.

This book is not carved in stone either. If there are other issues about the topic that you think I should address, please drop me a line, and I can always add it to the next edition.

hwrightwrighter@gmail.com

About the Author

Heather Wright is a freelance writer and part-time college instructor teaching business communications. Heather worked for many years in companies, both local and global in scope, and now runs her own freelance writing business. Through these experiences, she has developed her own communications skill set that she now shares in her Better Business Communications series and with her students, in the classroom, as well as in the workplace.

www.ingramcontent.com/pod-product-compliance
Lightning Source LLC
Chambersburg PA
CBHW070900180526
45168CB00005B/1882